PUFFIN BOOKS

EARLY IN THE MORNING

Nursery rhymes are a familiar, and yet mysterious, part of childhood. Where do they come from? They are a fascinating mix of ancient and modern verse, which combine to form a heritage linking generations of parents and children.

Early in the Morning is Charles Causley's marvellous contribution to this treasury of nursery rhymes. Charles Causley is a highly distinguished poet, and his forty new poems and rhymes blend perfectly the sound of traditional verse with his own intense originality. 'Round the corner comes Jack Fall', 'Mr Croco-doco-dile', 'Spin Me a Web, Spider' – Charles Causley's poems are full of the mysterious nonsense and haunting resonances that make nursery rhymes lodge in the back of the memory of everyone.

'A triumph . . . the long wait for a new volume of Causley's matchless children's poems has proved fully worthwhile. His writing here is full of joy and exuberance, as well as the familiar plangent note of loss and longing' – *Times Educational Supplement*

Charles Causley was born in Cornwall, where he still lives. After service in the Royal Navy he was for twenty-five years a schoolteacher before becoming a full-time writer. In 1967 he was awarded the Queen's Gold Medal for Poetry, and he is also a Fellow of the Royal Society of Literature. The University of Exeter conferred on him the honorary degree of Doctor of Letters in 1977. In the New Year Honours List for 1986 he was appointed CBE for his services to poetry.

Michael Foreman studied at the Royal College of Art. He has won many awards, including the Graphic Prize at Bologna, the Kurt Maschler Award and the Kate Greenaway Medal for 1982, and the Children's Book Award in 1984. He lives in London and Cornwall.

There is a hardback edition of *Early in the Morning* (published by Viking Kestrel) which includes music by Anthony Castro for twenty of the poems. The songs appear with full piano accompaniment and guitar chords. The book also includes full-colour illustrations by Michael Foreman.

PUFFIN BOOKS

Published by the Penguin Group
27 Wrights Lane, London w8 5TZ, England
Viking Penguin Inc., 40 West 23rd Street, New York, New York 10010, USA
Penguin Books Australia Ltd, Ringwood, Victoria, Australia
Penguin Books Canada Ltd, 2801 John Street, Markham, Ontario, Canada L3R 1B4
Penguin Books (NZ) Ltd, 182–190 Wairau Road, Auckland 10, New Zealand

Penguin Books Ltd, Registered Offices: Harmondsworth, Middlesex, England

First published (with colour) by Viking Kestrel 1986
Published in Puffin Books (black and white only) 1988
10 9 8 7 6 5 4 3 2

Made and printed in Great Britain by
Richard Clay Ltd, Bungay, Suffolk

Charles Causley

Early in the Morning

A COLLECTION OF NEW POEMS

Illustrated by Michael Foreman

PUFFIN BOOKS

Contents

Early in the Morning

Early in the morning
The water hits the rocks,
The birds are making noises
Like old alarum clocks,
The soldier on the skyline
Fires a golden gun
And over the back of the chimney-stack
Explodes the silent sun.

I Went to Santa Barbara

I went to Santa Barbara,
I saw upon the pier
Four-and-twenty lobster pots
And a barrel of German beer.

The ships in the bay sailed upside-down,
The trees went out with the tide,
The river escaped from the ocean
And over the mountain-side.

High on the hill the Mission
Broke in two in the sun.
The bell fell out of the turning tower
And struck the hour of one.

I heard a hundred fishes fly
Singing across the lake
When I was in Santa Barbara
And the earth began to shake.

My friend Gregor Antonio,
Was with me all that day,
Says it is all inside my head
And there's nothing in what I say.

But I was in Santa Barbara
And in light as bright as snow
I see it as if it were yesterday
Or a hundred years ago.

John Clark

John Clark sat in the park,
Saw the sun jump out of the dark,
Counted one and counted two,
Watched the sky from black to blue,
Counted three and counted four,
Heard a horse and then some more,
Counted five and counted six,
Heard a snapping in the sticks,
Counted seven and counted eight,
Saw a fox and saw his mate,
Counted nine and counted ten.

'Hurry home to your den, your den,
Or you never may see the sun again
For I fear I hear the hunting men,
The hunting men and the hounds that bark!'

Said John Clark as he sat in the park.

Spin Me a Web, Spider

Spin me a web, spider,
Across the window-pane
For I shall never break it
And make you start again.

Cast your net of silver
As soon as it is spun,
And hang it with the morning dew
That glitters in the sun.

It's strung with pearls and diamonds,
The finest ever seen,
Fit for any royal King
Or any royal Queen.

Would you, could you, bring it down
In the dust to lie?
Any day of the week, my dear,
Said the nimble fly.

Tommy Hyde

Tommy Hyde, Tommy Hyde,
What are you doing by the salt-sea side?

Picking up pebbles and smoothing sand
And writing a letter on the ocean strand.

Tommy Hyde, Tommy Hyde,
Why do you wait by the turning tide?

I'm watching for the water to rub it off the shore
And take it to my true-love in Baltimore.

There was an Old Woman

There was an old woman of Chester-le-Street
Who chased a policeman all over his beat.

She shattered his helmet and tattered his clothes
And knocked his new spectacles clean off his nose.

'I'm afraid,' said the Judge, 'I must make it quite clear
You can't get away with that sort of thing here.'

'I can and I will,' the old woman she said,
'And I don't give a fig for your water and bread.

'I don't give a hoot for your cold prison cell,
And your bolts and your bars and your handcuffs as well.

'I've never been one to do just as I'm bid.
You can put me in jail for a year!'
                                    So they did.

Mrs McPhee

Mrs McPhee
Who lived in South Zeal
Roasted a duckling
For every meal.

'Duckling for breakfast
And dinner and tea,
And duckling for supper,'
Said Mrs McPhee.

'It's sweeter than sugar,
It's clean as a nut,
I'm sure and I'm certain
It's good for me – BUT

'I don't like these feathers
That grow on my back,
And my silly webbed feet
And my voice that goes quack.'

As easy and soft
As a ship to the sea,
As a duck to the water
Went Mrs McPhee.

'I think I'll go swim
In the river,' said she;
Said Mrs Mac, Mrs Quack,
Mrs McPhee.

One for the Man

One for the man who lived by the sand,
Two for his son and daughter,
Three for the sea-birds washed so white
That flew across the water.

Four for the sails that brought the ship
About the headland turning.
Five for the jollyboys in her shrouds,
Six for the sea-lamps burning.

Seven for the sacks of silver and gold
They sailed through the winter weather.
Eight for the places set on shore
When they sat down together.

Nine for the songs they sang night-long,
Ten for the candles shining.
Eleven for the lawmen on the hill
As they all were sweetly dining.

Twelve for the hour that struck as they stood
To the Judge so careful and clever.
Twelve for the years that must come and go
And we shall see them never.

Daniel Brent

Daniel Brent, a man of Kent,
Went to market without a cent.
He chose an apple, he chose a pear,
He chose a comb for his crooked hair,
He chose a fiddle, he chose a flute,
He chose a rose for his Sunday suit,
He chose some pickles, he chose some ham,
He chose a pot of strawberry jam,
He chose a kite to climb the sky.

How many things did Daniel buy?

But when it came the time to pay,
Daniel Brent he ran away.

Freddie Phipps

Freddie Phipps
Liked fish and chips.
Jesse Pinch liked crime.

Woodrow Waters
Liked dollars and quarters.
Paul Small liked a dime.

Sammy Fink
Liked a lemon drink.
Jeremy Jones liked lime.

Mortimer Mills
Liked running down hills.
Jack Jay liked to climb.

Hamilton Hope
Liked water and soap.
Georgie Green liked grime;

But Willy Earls
Liked pretty girls
And had a much better time.

High on the Wall

High on the wall
Where the pennywort grows
Polly Penwarden
Is painting her toes.

One is purple
And two are red
And two are the colour
Of her golden head.

One is blue
And two are green
And the others are the colours
They've always been.

Wilbur

Wilbur, Wilbur,
Your bed is made of silver,
Your sheets are Irish linen,
Your pillow soft as snow.
Wilbur, Wilbur,
The girls all look you over,
Look you up and look you down
When into town you go.

Wilbur, Wilbur,
Walking by the river,
Swifter than the sunlight
Is your glancing eye.
Wilbur, Wilbur,
You're the sweetest singer.
You've a pair of dancing legs
That money cannot buy.

Wilbur, Wilbur,
On your little finger
You wear a ring of platinum
Set with a diamond stone.
But Wilbur, Wilbur,
Now the days are colder
You go to bed at six o'clock
And lie there all alone.

Charity Chadder

Charity Chadder
Borrowed a ladder,
Leaned it against the moon,
Climbed to the top
Without a stop
On the 31st of June,
Brought down every single star,
Kept them all in a pickle jar.

Jeremiah

Jeremiah
Jumped out of the fire
Into the frying pan;
Went zig and zag
With a sausage and egg
All the way to Japan.

But when he got
To Fuji-san
And saw the mountain smoking,
'Good gracious,' said he.
'This ain't for me';
Ran all the way back to Woking.

My Cat *Plumduff*

My cat Plumduff
When feeling gruff
Was terribly fond
Of taking snuff,
And his favourite spot
For a sniff and a sneeze
Was a nest at the very
Top of the trees.

And there he'd sit
And sneeze and sniff
With the aid of a gentleman's
Handkerchief;
And he'd look on the world
With a lordly air
As if he was master
Of everything there.

Cried the passers by,
'Just look at that!
He thinks he's a bird,
That silly old cat!'
But my cat Plumduff
Was heard to say,
'How curious people
Are today!'

'Do I think I'm a bird?'
Said my cat Plumduff.
'All smothered in fur
And this whiskery stuff,
With my swishy tail
And my teeth so sharp
And my guinea-gold eyes
That shine in the dark?

'Aren't they peculiar
People – and how!
Whoever has heard
Of a bird with a miaow?
Such ignorant creatures!
What nonsense and stuff!
No wonder I'm grumpy,'
Said my cat Plumduff.

Baby, Baby

Baby, baby
In the walking water,
Are you my sister's
Darling daughter?

My sister, they said,
Who went to Spain
And vowed she'd never
Come home again?

Her eyes were the self-same
Periwinkle-blue
And she wore a locket
Just like you.

She wore a shawl
Of Honiton lace
Like the one that drifts
About your face.

Baby, don't stray
Where the tall weeds swim.
Fetch the boat, Billy,
And bring the baby in.

The Owl Looked out of the Ivy Bush

The owl looked out of the ivy bush
And he solemnly said, said he,
'If you want to live an owlish life
Be sure you are not like me.

'When the sun goes down and the moon comes up
And the sky turns navy blue,
I'm certain to go tu-whoo tu-whit
Instead of tu-whit tu-whoo.

'And even then nine times out of ten
(And it's absolutely true)
I somehow go out of my owlish mind
With a whit-tu whoo-tu too.'

'There's nothing in water,' said the owl,
'In air or on the ground
With a kindly word for the sort of bird
That sings the wrong way round.'

'I might,' wept the owl in the ivy bush,
'Be just as well buried and dead.
You can bet your boots no one gives two hoots!'
'Do I, friend my,' I said.

Ring Dove

Ring dove, ring dove,
High in the tree,
What are the words
You say to me?

What do you sing
And what do you tell
Loud as the ring
Of a telephone bell?

Take two cows, Davy,
Take them to the shore,
And when you've taken two
Take two cows more.

At Linkinhorne *

At Linkinhorne
Where the devil was born
I met old Mollie Magee.
'Come in,' she said
With a wag of her head,
'For a cup of camomile tea.'
And while the water whistled and winked
I gazed about the gloom
At all the treasures Mollie Magee
Had up and down the room.

With a sort of a smile
A crocodile
Swam under an oaken beam,
And from tail to jaw
It was stuffed with straw
And its eye had an emerald gleam.
In the farthest corner a grandfather clock
Gave a watery tick and a tock
As it told the date and season and state
Of the tide at Falmouth Dock.

She'd a fire of peat
That smelled as sweet
As the wind from the moorland high,
And through the smoke
Of the chimney broke
A silver square of sky.
On the mantelshelf a pair of dogs
Gave a china smile and a frown,
And through the bottle-glass pane there stood
The church tower upside-down.

She'd shelves of books,
And hanging on hooks
Were herbals all to hand,
And shells and stones
And animal bones
And bottles of coloured sand.
And sharp I saw the scritch-owl stare
From underneath the thatch
As Matt her cat came through the door
With never a lifted latch.

At Linkinhorne
Where I was born
I met old Mollie Magee.
She told me this,
She told me that
About my family-tree.
And oh she skipped and ah she danced
And laughed and sang did we,
For Mollie Magee's the finest mother
Was ever given to me.

*Linkinhorne is a village in south-east Cornwall, and the first two lines of the poem are a well-known local saying.

In My Garden

In my garden
Grows a tree
Dances day
And night for me,
Four in a bar
Or sometimes three
To music secret
As can be.

Nightly to
Its hidden tune
I watch it move
Against the moon,
Dancing to
A silent sound,
One foot planted
In the ground.

Dancing tree,
When may I hear
Day or night
Your music clear?
What the note
And what the song
That you sing
The seasons long?

It is written,
Said the tree,
On the pages
Of the sea;
It is there
At every hand
On the pages
Of the land;

Whether waking
Or in dream:
Voice of meadow-grass
And stream,
And out of
The ringing air
Voice of sun
And moon and star.

It is there
For all to know
As tides shall turn
And wildflowers grow;
There for you
And there for me,
Said the glancing
Dancing tree.

Foxglove

Foxglove purple,
Foxglove white,
Fit for a lady
By day or night.

Foxglove bring
To friend and stranger
A witches' thimble
For the finger.

Foxglove on
The sailing sea,
Storm and tempest
There shall be.

Foxglove sleeping
Under the sky,
Watch the midnight
With one eye.

Foxglove burning
In the sun,
Ring your bells
And my day is done.

Stone in the Water

Stone in the water,
Stone on the sand,
Whom shall I marry
When I get to land?

Will he be handsome
Or will he be plain,
Strong as the sun
Or rich as the rain?

Will he be dark
Or will he be fair,
And what will be the colour
That shines in his hair?

Will he come late
Or will he come soon,
At morning or midnight
Or afternoon?

What will he say
Or what will he sing,
And will he be holding
A plain gold ring?

Stone in the water
Still and small,
Tell me if he comes,
Or comes not at all.

Round the Corner Comes Jack Fall

Round the corner comes Jack Fall,
Dressed in yellow, dressed in brown.
'Goodbye, summer,' hear him call
As he wanders through the town.

'Give her a kiss and wish her well,
Give her a gold and silver chain.
Tell her you love her,' said Jack Fall.
'And bring her back this way again.'

Said the Clown

Said the clown in the seven-ring circus
As he dived in a bucket of sand,
'Why nobody claps at my quips and my cracks
Is something I can't understand.

'The start of my act's a selection
Of millions and millions of jokes,
Then like wind and like fire I whizz down a wire
On a bike with one wheel and no spokes.

'When I fill up my pockets with water
And paint my face red, white and blue,
Folk stare at the ground and they don't make a sound.
I can't think of the reason. Can you?'

Mistletoe

Mistletoe new,
Mistletoe old,
Cut it down
With a knife of gold.

Mistletoe green,
Mistletoe milk,
Let it fall
On a scarf of silk.

Mistletoe from
The Christmas oak,
Keep my house
From lightning stroke.

Guard from thunder
My roof-tree
And any evil
That there be.

Janny Jim Jan

Janny Jim Jan
The Cornish man
Walked out on Bodmin Moor,
A twist of rye
For a collar and tie
And his boots on backsyvore. *

'Janny Jim Jan,'
The children sang,
'Here's a letter from the King of Spain.'
But Janny turned nasty,
Hit 'em with a pasty,
Sent 'em home again.

* the wrong way round

Balloono

Balloono, Balloono,
   What do you bring
Flying from your fingers
   And fifty bits of string?

Is it the sun
   Or is it the moon
Or is it a football
   For Saturday afternoon?

A peach or a melon?
   Tell me, please.
An orange or an apple
   Or a big Dutch cheese?

See them tugging
   In the bright blue air
As if they would wander
   Everywhere!

Come back, Balloono,
   When I draw my pay
And I'll buy them and fly them
   All away.

Take Me to the Water Fair

Take me to the Water Fair,
Row me in your boat,
Whisper with the willow tree
As down the stream we float.

The sky was cold as iron
When we set off from land,
But soon, you say, a day will come
With flowers on either hand.

Let me lie upon your arm
As on the flood we slide
And watch the shining fishes play
Swiftly our boat beside.

And here the lilies lean upon
The waters as we pass,
And there the munching cattle swim
Deep in the meadow grass.

As high above the chestnut burns
Its candles on the sky
You say that summer cannot end –
And you will never lie.

Nicholas Naylor

Nicholas Naylor
The deep-blue sailor
Sailed the sea
As a master-tailor.

He sewed for the Captain,
He sewed for the crew,
He sewed up the kit-bags
And hammocks too.

He sewed up a serpent,
He sewed up a shark,
He sewed up a sailor
In a bag of dark.

*How do you like
Your work, master-tailor?*
'So, so, so,'
Said Nicholas Naylor.

Rebekah

Rebekah, Rebekah,
Wake up from your sleep,
The cattle are thirsty
And so are the sheep
That come with the evening
Down from the high fell
To drink the sweet water
Of Paradise Well.

Rebekah, Rebekah,
The spring rises free
But the well it is locked
And you have the key,
And the sheep and the cattle
Rebekah, are dry
And would drink of the water.
And so would I.

John, John the Baptist

John, John the Baptist
Lived in a desert of stone,
He had no money,
Ate beans and honey,
And he lived quite on his own.

His coat was made of camel,
His belt was made of leather,
And deep in the gleam
Of a twisting stream
He'd stand in every weather.

John, John the Baptist
Worked without any pay,
But he'd hold your hand
And bring you to land
And wash your fears away.

Tell, Tell the Bees

Tell, tell the bees,
The bees in the hive,
That Jenny Green is gone away,
Or nothing will thrive.

There'll be no honey
And there'll be no comb
If you don't tell the bees
That Jenny's not home.

Tap on their window,
Tap on their door,
Tell them they'll never see
Jenny Green more.

Tell them as true
As you know how
Who is their master
Or mistress now.

Tell all the hives
As they buzz and hum,
Jenny is gone
But another will come.

Tell, tell the bees,
The bees in the hive,
That Jenny Green is gone away,
Or nothing will thrive.

I Love My Darling Tractor

I love my darling tractor,
I love its merry din,
Its muscles made of iron and steel,
Its red and yellow skin.

I love to watch its wheels go round
However hard the day,
And from its bed inside the shed
It never thinks to stray.

It saves my arm, it saves my leg,
It saves my back from toil,
And it's merry as a skink when I give it a drink
Of water and diesel oil.

I love my darling tractor
As you can clearly see,
And so, the jolly farmer said,
Would you if you were me.

Let's Go Ride

Let's go ride in a sleigh, Johanna,
Let's go ride in a sleigh,
Through the mountains,
Under the trees,
Over the ice
On Lake Louise.
Let's go ride in a sleigh, Johanna,
       – There's only five dollars to pay.

Let's go ride today, Johanna,
Let's go ride today,
The horses shaking
Their silver traces,
The branches flaking
Snow on our faces.
Let's go ride today, Johanna,
       – There's only five dollars to pay.

Let's go ride while we may, Johanna,
Let's go ride while we may,
By the tall ice-fall
And the frozen spring
As the frail sun shines
And the sleigh-bells ring.
Let's go ride while we may, Johanna,
    – There's only five dollars to pay.

Johnny Come over the Water

Johnny come over the water
And make the sun shine through.
Johnny come over the water
And paint the sky with blue.

Cover the field and the meadow
With flowers of red and gold,
And cover with leaves the simple trees
That stand so bare and cold.

Johnny come over the water,
Turn the white grass to hay.
It's winter, winter all the year
Since you went away.

Here's the Reverend Rundle

Here's the Reverend Rundle
His gear in a bundle,
He has a dog
He has a sled
And thousands of stories
In his head
And coloured pictures
Of the Holy Scriptures
To show, show
The Indians red
Who had picture and story
And saints in glory
And a heavenly throne
Of their very own
But were so well-bred
That they met him like a brother
And they loved each other
It was said,
The Reverend Rundle
And the Indians red
And through the Rockies
They watched him go
Over the ice
And under the snow –
But this was a very long
Time ago,
A long, long, long, long
Time ago.

They loved him from
His heels to his hat
As he rode on the rough
Or walked on the flat
Whether he stood
Or whether he sat,
The Reverend Rundle
His gear in a bundle
And as well as that
His favourite cat
Warm in a poke
Of his sealskin cloak
For fear some son
Of a hungry gun

Ate her for supper
In Edmonton
And they loved each other
It was said,
The Reverend Rundle
And the Indians red
And through the Rockies
They watched him go
Over the ice
And under the snow –
But this was a very long
Time ago,
A long, long, long, long
Time ago.

The Money Came in, Came in

My son Sam was a banjo man,
His brother played the spoons,
Willie Waley played the ukelele
And his sister sang the tunes:
  Sometimes sharp,
  Sometimes flat,
  It blew the top
  Off your Sunday hat,
  But no one bothered
  At a thing like that,
  And the money came in,
    came in.

Gussie Green played a tambourine,
His wife played the mandolin,
Tommy Liddell played a one-string
    fiddle
He made from a biscuit tin.
            Sometimes flat,
            Sometimes sharp,
            The noise was enough
            To break your heart,
            But nobody thought
            To cavil or carp,
            And the money came in,
                came in.

Clicketty Jones she played the bones,
Her husband the kettle-drum,
Timothy Tout blew the inside out
Of a brass euphonium.
    Sometimes sharp,
    Sometimes flat,
    It sounded like somebody
    Killing the cat,
    But no one bothered
    At a thing like that,
    And the money came in,
        came in.

Samuel Shute he played the flute,
His sister played the fife.
The Reverend Moon played a double
    bassoon
With the help of his lady wife.
            Sometimes flat,
            Sometimes sharp
            As a pancake
            Or an apple tart,
            But everyone, everyone
            Played a part
            And the money came in,
                came in.

Good Morning, Mr Croco-doco-dile

Good morning, Mr Croco-doco-dile,
And how are you today?
I like to see you croco-smoco-smile
In your croco-woco-way.

From the tip of your beautiful croco-
    toco-tail
To your croco-hoco-head
You seem to me so croco-stoco-still
As if you're croco-doco-dead.

Perhaps if I touch your croco-cloco-claw
Or your croco-snoco-snout,
Or get up close to your croco-joco-jaw
I shall very soon find out.

But suddenly I croco-soco-see
In your croco-oco-eye
A curious kind of croco-gloco-
    gleam,
So I just don't think I'll try.

Forgive me, Mr Croco-doco-dile
But it's time I was away.
Let's talk a little croco-woco-while
Another croco-doco-day.

When I was a Boy

When I was a boy
On the Isle of Wight
We all had a bath
On Friday night.
The bath was made
Of Cornish tin
And when one got out
Another got in.
    First there was Jenny
    Then there was Jean,
    Then there was Bessie
    Skinny as a bean,
    Then there was Peter,
    Then there was Paul,
    And I was the very last
    One of all.

When mammy boiled the water
We all felt blue
And we lined up like
A cinema queue.
We never had time
To bob or blush
When she went to work
With the scrubbing brush.
    First there was Jenny, etc.

When I was a boy
On the Isle of Wight
My mammy went to work
Like dynamite:
Soap on the ceiling,
Water on the floor,
Mammy put the kettle on
And boil some more!
        First there was Jenny, etc.

I am the Song

I am the song that sings the bird.
I am the leaf that grows the land.
I am the tide that moves the moon.
I am the stream that halts the sand.
I am the cloud that drives the storm.
I am the earth that lights the sun.
I am the fire that strikes the stone.
I am the clay that shapes the hand.
I am the word that speaks the man.